Under My Feet

# Moles

## Patricia Whitehouse

Raintree

**www.raintreepublishers.co.uk**
Visit our website to find out more information about **Raintree** books.

To order:
☎ Phone 44 (0) 1865 888112
🖹 Send a fax to 44 (0) 1865 314091
🖥 Visit the Raintree Bookshop at **www.raintreepublishers.co.uk** to browse our catalogue and order online.

First published in Great Britain by Raintree, Halley Court, Jordan Hill, Oxford OX2 8EJ, part of Harcourt Education.
Raintree is a registered trademark of Harcourt Education Ltd.

Editorial: Diyan Leake and Kate Buckingham
Design: Sue Emerson and Michelle Lisseter
Picture Research: Jennifer Gillis
Production: Jonathan Smith

Originated by Dot Gradations
Printed and bound in China by South China Printing Company

ISBN 1 844 43731 0
08 07 06 05 04
10 9 8 7 6 5 4 3 2 1

**British Library Cataloguing in Publication Data**
Whitehouse, Patricia
Moles
599.3'35
A full catalogue record for this book is available from the British Library.

**Acknowledgements**
The publishers would like to thank the following for permission to reproduce photographs: Bruce Coleman Inc. pp. 17, 20, 23 (Hans Reinhard); Corbis pp. 11L, 16 (Jeffrey L. Rotman), 23; DRK Photo, p. 13 (D. Cavagnaro); Dwight Kuhn pp. 8, 15, 18, 19, 21; Earth Scenes pp. 6 (Marian Bacon), 23; Getty Images pp. 4 (Digital Vision), 11R (C. McIntyre); Oxford Scientific Films p.7; Photo Researchers Inc. pp.5 (Gregory K. Scott), 9, 10, 23 (Steve Maslowski), 12, 23 (Jean Philippe); Visuals Unlimited p. 14 (Leonard Lee Rue III); Illustration on page 22 by William Hobbs.

Cover photograph reproduced with permission of Photo Researchers Inc./OKAPIA/Manfred Danegger.

Every effort has been made to contact copyright holders of any material reproduced in this book. Any omissions will be rectified in subsequent printings if notice is given to the publishers.

Some words are shown in bold, **like this.**
You can find them in the glossary on page 23.

# Contents

# Do moles live here?

Have you ever seen a mole?

When you go outside, you might be walking over one!

Moles live under your feet.

Their homes are underground.

# What are moles?

Moles are **mammals**.

All mammals have hair or fur on their bodies.

Mammals make milk for
their babies.

These are young baby moles.

# What do moles look like?

claw | eye | paw

Moles have two tiny eyes.

They have short legs and big front paws with long claws.

snout

Moles have long **snouts** and pointed teeth.

Most moles are about the size of a kitten.

# Where do moles live?

Most moles live alone.

Their homes are called **burrows**.

Some moles live in places with trees or rivers.

Other moles live in **deserts**.

# What do mole homes look like?

Most mole homes have special rooms for sleeping.

The rooms are joined by **tunnels**.

Some mole homes have many tunnels.

You can see the tunnel ridges above the ground.

# How do moles find their way?

Most moles cannot see well.

This kind of mole cannot see at all.

Moles use their noses to smell.

This mole has special parts on its nose that help it to find food.

# How do moles make their homes?

Moles use their front paws to dig **tunnels** underground.

They push the soil outside.

The soil piles up around the holes.

These piles of soil are called **molehills**. Have you ever seen one?

# What is special about mole homes?

Moles use their **tunnels** to trap food.

**Insects** and worms fall through the soil into the tunnels.

The mole walks along the tunnels to find insects and worms.

Then the mole eats them.

# When do moles come out from underground?

Most moles do not come out of their **burrows**.

They cannot move quickly or see above ground.

Some moles come out to find food.

The mole in this picture is
swimming to find food!

# Mole home map

tunnel ridge

molehill

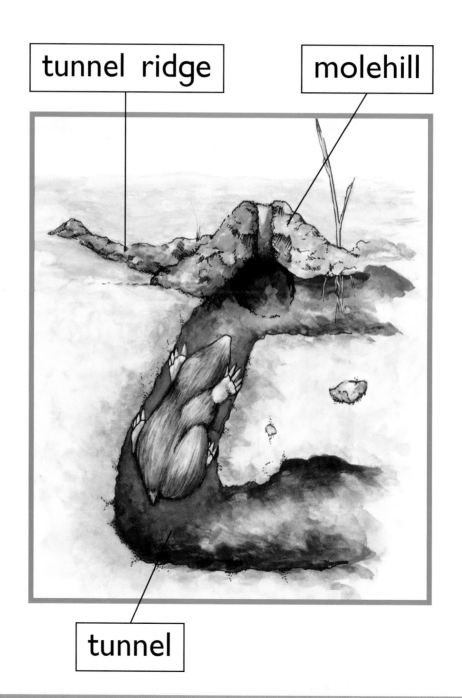

tunnel